MARQUETTA HEWITT

Stop! Fix Your Marketing Now

The Marketing Handbook for Freelancers, Entrepreneurs, and Startups

This book is dedicated to everyone who will ever have an idea. Anyone who has ever had an idea and anyone who may have stolen an idea. Co-creation is a magical and exciting thing. We don't always know how we will create what we want, but we always know what we want to create. I wrote this book to show you it is always possible.

Contents

Acknowledgement

I want to thank my closest friends and family for inspiring me to continue to have confidence in all that I do. It is not always easy but it is always worth it.

1

Introduction

Hello my fellow **Tycoon**! Let me introduce myself, my name is Marquetta Hewitt. I am a long-time entrepreneur and creative. I have a passion for helping others create and thrive confidently in their business and life. Through the years I have had the pleasure of meeting and interacting with some of the most amazing minds on the planet. My journey has led me to understand that the success we seek is inherently tied to how well we visualize, receive, and implement information.

A few years ago, I used to listen to a YouTube Channel that focused on enhancing and cultivating the highly creative power that exists within our minds. In the intro there was a guy that said, "The hottest commodity is information". That line has since stuck with me as a reminder that my knowledge and experience is indeed a valuable asset that I can use to obtain whatever I want in life. Through my journey I have also learned that success is not just about how hard you work, it is also about how you feel, how you receive, and how you implement information. We are currently in the age of Aquarius, now is a prime time to manifest your wildest dreams. To state it simply, the stars are practically aligned to support you in whatever you decide to move towards accomplishing. All that is needed is a strong desire to see it through, a willingness to learn, exercising wisdom to make informed decisions and taking inspired action.

The purpose of this book is to provide you, my fellow Tycoon, with the information needed to see your successful idea thrive in 2021 and beyond. I have spent the last several years learning about marketing, sales and entrepreneurship. Throughout my years of entrepreneurship I never understood how important marketing was until I joined a mentorship last year to become a **business coach**. I learned so much and I have been in awe at how much is possible with a concept called brand or "value based" marketing. Even though brand marketing is imperative and should be a hot topic, it is a subject that I do not hear come up often when discussions around business take place. In many business groups I have joined, the conversations usually revolve around how to make the sale, how to grow followings on social media, or where to run ads for your business. Observing and having conversations with freelancers, entrepreneurs, and startups, I constantly hear them express frustration and overwhelm about the challenges that come with trying to understand and succeed in the marketing of their brand. Determining where to start and how to implement a good marketing strategy is a pressing challenge for most of them. Even the questions I receive over and over again are usually concerns about how to connect with their target audience, how to increase sales, and build a successful thriving brand. I advise many of them to reach out to their audiences in a way that makes them feel valued and a part of something bigger. I mention how it is important to make a genuine effort to connect with your audience by highlighting what makes your brand a great thing to be associated with. Your marketing is how you present your brand as whole to the world through creating experiences, ideas, emotions and conversations .

This book will guide you on how to present your brand the world through what is known as brand marketing. My goal with this book is to break down brand marketing and make it far less intimidating for freelancers, entrepreneurs, and startups. You will completely understand what brand marketing is and how to implement it in your business. We will discuss key note topics such as your brand story, target audience, success fundamentals, the importance of value and briefly mention several types of marketing. I have also included within this book a step-by-step outline for devising your very own marketing strategy. You will have the information you need to create great brand marketing to produce a successful brand that thrives for the long term.

I believe that everyone can be successful at whatever it is they choose to do. I call you a Tycoon because you are a person of great influence, power, and wealth. You have the resources within yourself to create magnificent things. You just have to make the choice to follow through once you receive this information. Do not just read this book and do nothing, use this book as a tool for imminent success. I am sharing this information because there is a large demand for it, and with all that I have been fortunate to learn I feel obligated to deliver that knowledge to you. It is my way of contributing to a progressive and value based world that is my hope for the future of brands. To the individual now reading this, you could have the next big great idea that would change the world, but you need to know how to market that idea. I write this book in hopes that it motivates you to keep going and to see it all the way through no matter what. Do not let something as small as lack of knowledge stop you. Just learn what you need to know, implement the information and more importantly ask for help if you need it! I am glad to speak with you or offer additional resources and assistance. My information is located in the back of this book, feel free to reach out if you have any questions.

To Your Success,
　　Marquetta Hewitt
　　Creative Entrepreneur

2

Chapter 1: What is Marketing?

In my attempts at creating many brand ideas and concepts over the years, I never realized or understood how important marketing was. In fact, I had no clue that it was the one component I needed to ensure I was successful in any type of brand I would create. I was completely ignorant to the idea of what it takes to really draw in an audience and convert them into customers. Which is why I failed miserably, but now that I have come to study and understand marketing, I can relay to you its significance. **Marketing** is one of the most misunderstood and overlooked concepts when it comes to establishing a brand. Generally the concept of marketing is defined as "actions a company takes to promote the buying and or selling of a product or service." In my own words I define marketing as "putting together a strategy to generate leads, convert them into customers, while also building awareness, credibility, loyalty and culture within and around your brand".

There are many variations of definitions that encompass what marketing is, but simply put, it is how you host and interact with your audience in hopes that they become avid customers of your product or service. Over time technology has opened up to us channels to interact with people in a multitude of ways. The increased usage of computers, cellphones, and live streaming applications make connecting with potential customers a much faster and easier process than years and years ago. There are several subcategories that exist in the realm of marketing such as content, influencer,digital, and brand marketing.

Content marketing is creating, publishing, and distributing content in the form of videos, written format, and audio format to promote and sell a product or service. **Influencer marketing** is collaborating with a well-known authoritative individual or brand to promote your product or service. The most common and recognizable form of influencer marketing is celebrity endorsement. **Digital marketing** is using online based technology such as computers and phones to promote and sell a product or service. **Brand marketing** is the theory and tactics used to promote your brand overall by giving value to the customer. Each method when combined becomes a powerful arsenal when implemented into a long-term marketing strategy.

A **marketing strategy** is a plan of action to promote or sell a product or service. The objective of a marketing strategy is to facilitate the buying process by either providing quality informative content (value) and/or by executing strategic advertising campaigns. When done successfully it creates brand credibility and formulates a competitive advantage in the marketplace. As a result of providing quality content, people begin to view the brand as an authority figure in its industry. When brands make it a priority to provide quality content via marketing with consistency, it position the brand as a credible source or authority. In exchange for providing quality content, trust and loyalty is gained from the audience. Once trust is established the audience is more open and willing to buy the brand's products and services. This is due to the brand producing value to its audience instead of constantly asking for the sale.

Content Marketing

Digital Marketing

Influencer Marketing

As an essential component of communication to the customer or audience, marketing contributes a large part to the success and longevity of a brand. What is a brand exactly? To make it simple and easy to understand **Brand** is defined as the symbol, name, term, design, or any other features that uniquely identifies and distinguishes a company. It can also be described as the overall percieved set of expectations and standards that is associated with the brand and recognized by others. Brand marketing is a method of marketing used to ensure that a brand continues to connect with its audience over and throughout time. It is apparent that for your business to thrive and have longevity, you will need customers, happy ones, and ones that will continue to buy from you for life. When done in the right way brand marketing reflects a lifestyle, philosophy, and sense of community tied to your brand. It connects with your audience on an emotional and relatable level. It also might imply or project a certain standard of value. Think about it like this, we all have everyday challenges that we face and do our best to overcome. Everyone has problems no matter how unique or different, we still share commonality with all people that live and breathe on the planet we call earth. When your audience feels that you understand who they are and that they are valued, they are more likely to want to get to know you, trust you and spend their money with you.

Additionally, to truly emerge your brand or to successfully differentiate your brand, you need to have some form of a marketing strategy in place. It must be an essential unit of your business plan if you want to be around long-term. Today, so many opportunities exist to market your brand when you take into account channels such as social media and content sharing platforms. Millions of users exist on these platforms logging in every single day looking to solve a problem they have or obtain a result they want. It is no secret that most people shop online, have an email address, and participate on at least one social media platform.

Think With Google reported that **78%** of consumers have spent more time researching a brand or product online than they have researching in a store. So just think about the opportunity you now have to market your product or service and also consistently get in front of people who are looking for what you have to offer. This is where you zoom in on the marketing. Prioritize finding your audience amongst those millions and millions of people because amongst the crowd is a group that is looking for what you have to offer. Keep in mind that the possibilities for the methods of marketing online are plentiful. As technology and platforms continue to grow, more and more businesses are realizing the power of brand marketing and are creating strategies to engage and facilitate the buying process of their products and services. Here are some amazing and eye-opening statistics to add some perspective on how impactful marketing has become today with the technology and platforms available.

48% of companies are spending between 4-10% of their revenue on marketing Source: Hook Agency

50%+ of companies say the highest return on investment activities are search-related– including paid search, SEO and content marketing. Source: Hook Agency

44.4% of companies said that their top marketing objective was to increase lead generation. Source: Hook Agency

84% of people expect brands to produce content that entertains, provides solutions, and produces experiences and events.
Source: Meaningful Brands

The average user will spend **88%** more time on a website with video content goes to show that long-form videos can help keep people interested in your message and your brand. Source: Oberlo

72% of people preferring to learn about a company via video rather than text. Source: Wyzeowl

With just this small amount of insight you can certainly understand why it is crucial that you create some form of your own marketing strategy for your business. It is much easier now than ever before to create marketing content and advertising. Many specifically designed user-friendly software and platforms are becoming easily and readily accessible. If you are looking to create **advertising** and content to introduce your brand to an audience, you no longer have to go through a big corporate company or purchase an expensive software suite to do it. You can easily create ads and content by yourself with budget friendly SaaS (Software As A Service) platforms. You may even consider hiring a part-time employee, or hire a freelancer for the specific task that you need.

Developing a successful marketing strategy will require some dedicated time and detailed planning. To have a thriving brand, people must know your brand exists. As a brand, when you invest the time and quality it takes to create strong marketing, the return brings extremely successful results. With so many products and tools to choose from, deciding on the ones best for your brand can be overwhelming. To help the process flow easier some self reflection is required in order to properly select brand priorities. The key to making the process less complicated and overwhelming is to start small. Do not attempt to do every type of marketing or use every platform at once. Do diligent research to find out what platforms and methods will work best for your brand. Write down ideas and come up with a clear solid plan of action. Once you have your plan of action, think about how your brand can be influential and helpful to your audience with quality content.

Currently, people are expecting a lot more from brands when asked about what they are willing to accept on the subject of service and value. Customer service and customer retention reign as one of many major focuses for establishing a high performing brand. Creating a marketing strategy that ensures the needs of your audience are being met is a proactive way to stay on top of your game. Many brands today lack knowledge about the power that comes with brand marketing. Some positive results of brand marketing are having endless customers to introduce products to and making so many sales you may not be able to keep up. Often, I have observed brands only doing the bare minimum or nothing at all with their marketing. Failing to establish a marketing presence hurts the authority, credibility and overall image of your brand. We create our brand as a means to one day be self sustaining, we are all in business to see some type of return on our investment. However, be sure not to lose sight of how important it is to reinvest in your brand by providing substantial quality and value. Failure to do so may cause loss of traction, interest, and sometimes trust with the audience of your brand. Think of marketing as a regular investment for your brand and be proactive about its longevity and success. Consider what the consequences are when only personal or lackful-mindset interests are made the priority. When faced with making decisions about the direction or expansion of your brand, think of how those choices may affect the overall image of your brand. Take into consideration the audience you currently serve and how they may be impacted as well as the consistency of your brand.

For example, cutting back on a particular product because you want to switch it out with a cheaper one may not be a good move. Sacrificing quality for quantity is very enticing but consider the benefits of being quality driven in your brand. It will set you apart in your industry and drive up the value of your brand. Granted, we cannot always please everyone or be driven astray by the audience but it helps to keep the focus on what really matters when you consider the people you serve. People appreciate value and authenticity so be sure to create products, services, brand marketing, and brand culture that reflect those concepts in the best way.

Let's discuss **brand culture** as it pertains to marketing. When I refer to brand culture I am referring to the sense of lifestyle, habits, and etiquette associated with your brand and the people who are a part of it. Brand culture can also refer to activities or services that make your brand outstandingly recognizable.

For example, I recently picked up the hobby of electric skateboarding. There is one particular company, I will call them Company A that is known for its outstanding after-sales customer service. I do not own an electric skateboard from Company A but because of the word of mouth marketing from their consumer base about their customer service, I look forward to making my next purchase from them. It is something that makes them uniquely stand out among some other popular known brands. Many of those popular brands often receive complaints about lackluster after-sales service. Company A can market their after-sales customer service as a benefit of purchasing an electric skateboard with their brand. Along with the reviews of positive interaction with prior customers. Future buyers will be excited and confident in making a purchase from Company A knowing that they will not be abandoned after the sale.

Lastly, it is also imperative that your business has a story to tell about how it came to be, its values, and its philosophies. Having a brand story will help you establish your brand culture and help attract an audience who feels connected to your brand. Your story tells who your brand is for and what you stand for as a company. It draws people into feeling included and gives them an opportunity to relate, feel appreciated and a part of a larger community. Being connected is something that makes us all human and many brands have failed to recognize this through out the years. The brands that are doing it right opinion are treating people as an integral part of their brand. They show genuine care and concern and are helpful by providing quality information, products, and services. They use marketing to demonstrate and communicate their brand's culture, lifestyle, value and mission to their audience . Many brands have made it an essential goal in their business plans to establish marketing teams dedicated to focusing on the audience of their brand. Brands that dedicate time and focus on their marketing tend to see better results on **customer acquisition** and **customer retention.**

3

Chapter 2: What is Branding?

One of a few ways to gauge if marketing efforts will be successful is through the presence (or lack there of) of branding. **Branding** helps to shape and cultivate how customers will view your company in its entirety. Branding is defined as the promotion of a particular product or company by means of advertising and distinctive design. The key word here that I want to highlight is "distinctive".

With so many companies in the marketplace and more entering every single day, you should aim to do more than the status quo to stand out. In my opinion this is not difficult to do if you are willing to do your research and put some serious thought into your brand. Many new **freelancers, entrepreneurs,** and **startups** fail in their efforts to produce a successful brand because they completely skip out on establishing the branding. They immediately rush to have a product to sell, or jump the gun to eagerly be seen without investment into three essential concepts that contribute to strong branding.

Those three things are:

1. **Brand Image**
2. **Brand Identity**
3. **Brand Marketing**

Your brands image, identity, and marketing are segments that work together to create the avatar of your brand. It is used to project the overall feelings, emotions, views, and attitudes that people will connect to your brand. Put time and care into each of these areas so that your branding promotes a positive reputation. Let's dive a little deeper into these concepts a little more.

Brand Image

Brand image is the impression of your product and brand that current or future customers have. It refers to the mind of the customer and is directly related to the feelings, thoughts, and ideas that they hold in regards to your brand. Every interaction that someone has with your brand cultivates its image. What are the types of feelings, thoughts, and ideas your brand image triggers? Do those perceptions directly align with the overall values and mission of your brand? This is something to evaluate and make the necessary changes if needed to influence a desired outcome. It can be a challenge to create a consistent and positive brand image because every person will have varying interactions with your brand. Counteract the negative interactions by making a genuine effort to understand and listen to what customers have to say about your brand. Use that information to improve the customer experience and cultivate a positive brand image. This is what will attract new customers, help you to introduce new products, and inspire confidence with existing customers. A negative brand image can undesirably affect the potential to reach new customers and launch new products. Something to consider when spending time, effort and resources to influence a positive outlook on your brand image.

Brand Identity

Brand identity refers to the visible aspects of your brand such as the logo, color scheme, and design. Often times brand indentity is thought of being the same as brand image, but they are not the same.

Let's say we are building a house, think of identity as being the bricks and the house as being the image. The identity or bricks are individual components that are placed strategically and each one should emit a high degree of quality. When the bricks are of high quality the house will stand strong. However, if the bricks are not of high quality, and contain eroded or broken pieces then the stability of the house is threatened. So when it comes to your brand the bricks you apply to make up your identity should be of high quality. Let's say the bricks of your brand might be your brand's logo, an eye-catching cohesive color scheme, and a clean consistent design. Each of those bricks should possess high quality with the least amount of erosion and broken parts for the house or image to look great. If one or perhaps all of the bricks are broken, inconsistent, or missing then the house or image looks incomplete, unappealing, or rundown.

The bricks that make up your brand identity should strategically portray how you want to be seen by current and future customers. The identity of your brand is something that you have complete control over. However, when it comes to your brand image, this is something that is created and promoted by the customer. Being proactive with the things you can control sets the tone and standard for how your brand will be perceived.

Brand Marketing

Brand Marketing is the technique used with communications, products, service and sales that allows your brand to grow exponentially. Investing in brand marketing elevates the value of your brand and company as a whole (**equity**). The concept is to market your brand's key values to build an overall positive impression to customers. Brand marketing does take more time, because it is something that is built by demonstrating the values of your brand through customer interaction. It entails being strategic about conveying your brand's identity, values, and personality through communication (content or advertising). This is why many companies may choose to focus on short term goals that get immediate results.

This tactic is better known as **Direct Response Marketing** (DRM). Direct Response Marketing relies on an immediate response to an offer presented through advertising. It is very popular because it often takes little to no time to see measurable results. Many freeleancers, entrepreneurs, and startups most commonly utilize this method of marketing. Depending on how DRM is used, it can sabotage and disparage a brand in the long run because they have no real sustainable relationship with the customer. It tends to go like this, get in, get the sale, get the next sale and repeat. It often leads to brands making grandiose promises or offering discounts in order to drive a high level of response. As well as having to continue to spend on advertising efforts to keep a consistent stream of customers.

Despite the extended timeline that comes with choosing to invest in brand marketing as a priority, the benefit of doing so solidifies the customer relationship, displays value, and creates trust. Therefore expanding the overall perceived value of your brand, increasing customer loyalty and subsquently brand equity and **revenue**.

The intention of your brand marketing should aim to do five things:

1. Create a positive response.
2. Give clear product information and ask for customer feedback.
3. Close the sale.
4. Teach your customers how to properly use your product to get the most value from it.
5. Reconnect with existing customers to determine the durability of the value.

5 Objectives of Brand Marketing

1. Create a positive response.

2. Give clear product information and ask for customer feedback.

3. Close the sale.

4. Teach your customers how to properly use the product for the most value.

5. Reconnect with customers to determine the durability of the value.

Establishing these five components in your brand marketing will create an ongoing relationship between your brand and customers. It promotes repeat buying, creates loyal customers, and collectively strengthens your branding. In the next chapter we will dicuss a concept that relates to brand image which is brand personality.

Chapter 3: Who, What, Where and Who?

A successful brand is one that continues to evolve, grow, expand, satisfy its customers, and increase revenue. To achieve these milestones there is some information you must take time to provide that will be essential for communicating your brand personality to the marketplace. You will need to effectively explain four things. These four things are what I call the **Brand Personality Code**:

1. Who Are You?
2. What Do You Do?
3. Who Do You Help?
4. How Do You Do What You Do?

Brand Personality Code

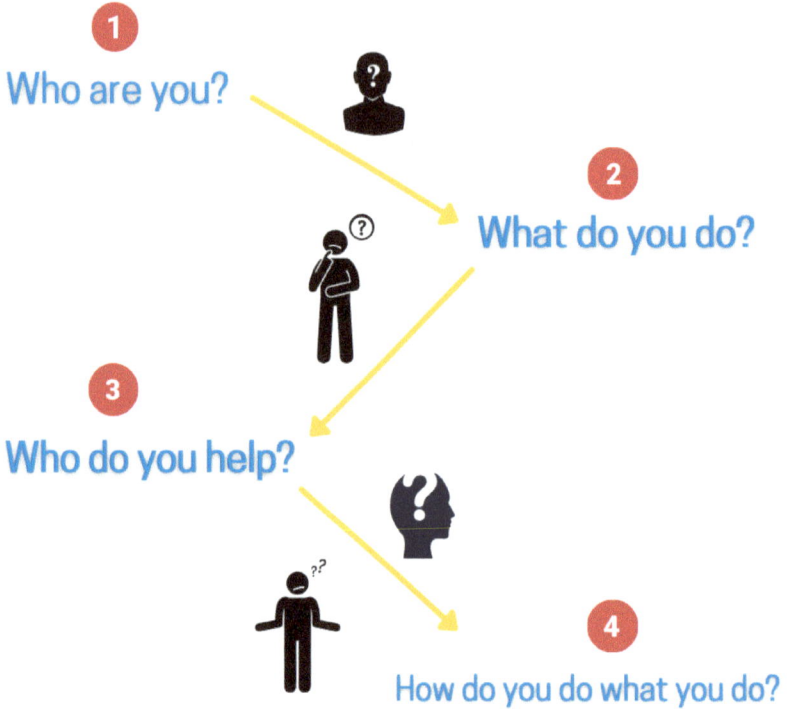

1 Who are you?

2 What do you do?

3 Who do you help?

4 How do you do what you do?

Answering these four questions in your marketing will ensure that you reach and communicate with your target audience. Clarifying information about your brand in these four areas will attract customers who are more suited to like and buy your product or service. The brand personality code helps you create a filter so that your marketing is more defined and helps your audience understand who your brand is for. The more concise and clear you are about these four areas the more accurate you will be when targeting your audience with brand marketing.

Who Are You?

People want to know what your brand is about, where you came from, and how your product or service came to be. Answering these question helps create your brand story. Take a moment to sit down and think about the thoughts and actions that led you to creating your business. Think about how you might be able to make it motivational, intriguing, interesting, or emotionally captivating. It can also be helpful to ask others such as family, friends and even strangers their thoughts about you and your brand. What do they see when they look at your brand and what is the energy that they feel? The feedback will help you better define the reasoning behind your brand and the way you want to be perceived by future customers.

For example, a vegan ice-cream shop tells a story of how they wanted to create an animal free alternative ice-cream. The owner was inspired during their journey of becoming a vegan and decided to open a vegan ice-cream shop to help spread awareness for animal causes. In their brand marketing they declare that a percentage of their profits are donated to animal charities as a way to support the cause of animals. With their story they are able to invoke an emotional interest as well as intrigue the audience. People who love and support animals will be drawn to learn more about the brand. They are more likely to become customers because they have something in common wit the vegan ice-cream shop, a love for animals.

People that are seeking alternative options for ice cream for diety reasons would also be another target market for the vegan ice-cream shop. Using brand marketing the vegan ice-cream shop has positioned itself as a health conscious and mindful brand looking to make a positive impact on the world. It will be thought of as a place worth spending your hard-earned money because you know it will also go to a good cause. This is an example of how a story makes an impact in how people connect with and support your brand.

What Do You Do?

The sophistication is in the simplicity. Answer this question by stating exactly what it is your company does. If you are a fashion designer say you make (insert adjective) clothes, if you are an author say you write (insert adjective) books, if you are a makeup artist say you apply (insert adjective) makeup on faces. The key here is to say what it is you actually do, not who you are. Two reasons behind this idea is that 1) it puts an image in the prospective customers mind and 2) the title for a particular skill or industry may not always convey what is actually being done. Sometimes people may be looking for a product or service and just are not aware that there is a specific name for it. By saying what it is that you actually do you keep it simple and easy to understand for potential customers. There are so many questions that may go unanswered when you are not clear about what you do. People make assumptions all the time, and may have limiting beliefs about certain skills or industries or are simply unaware to what it may actually involve.

For example, an esthetician who is marketing their business should not only say that they are an esthetician. They should make it a point to say what they actually do, which is perform cosmetic skin treatments. My first time hearing about estheticians I had no idea what that was, but I do have a general understanding of what cosmetic skin treatments are.

Another example I will use is a personal trainer. When most people think of a personal trainer, they think about a hard grueling intense workout consisting of pushups and long runs on a treadmill. Instead of saying "I'm a personal trainer" you might more accurately state the type of workout or areas of the body you help people improve. Always be direct when you tell people what it is you do. Leave no room for them to wonder and think, "okay I kind of know what that is but what exactly do they do?"

Who Do You Help?

The most important phase of constructing effective communication of your brand personality is knowing who you help. Look to your brand story of who you are, as well as what you do, and how you do it to answer this effectively. This is where it counts because if you do not know who you want to help you essentially have no audience to market to. That means you have no customers, no sales, and no revenue for your business. The people you will help are looking for two things. They want a result that they have not been able to achieve or they want a solution for a problem they have not solved.

Here is an example:

A woman is searching numerous online clothing boutiques in search of a perfect dress. However, she is not confident that she will find the right size as she becomes confused about the sizing charts provided on many of the websites that she visits. She gets frustrated by this, takes a break and ponders on what she can do. She has an event to attend in a couple of months and wanted to secure a dress as soon as possible. She does not want to worry about doing any shopping at the last minute. She often complains to her friends about how she can never find anything to fit her exactly right. She jokingly exclaims that she may need to find someone that can make her dresses personally. This woman would be an ideal customer for a designer but not just any designer. A custom dress designer who helps women who are frustrated with the online shopping experience when it comes to ordering dresses that will fit exactly right. Women who fit this description are more than likely the type of people a custom dress designer would aim to help.

Here is another example:

A professional boxer has been doing intense workouts five days a week in order to move up a weight class. He has been doing his current trainer's recommended workouts but is not seeing the results that he would like. His current workout routine does not have any specially designed excercises that help him accomplish his weight goal. The boxer expresses to a friend that he needs to find a different trainer who understands his problem and has a soution on how to help him reach his weight goal. The boxer would be the ideal client for a personal trainer but not just any personal trainer. A personal trainer that specializes in muscle mass who helps serious athletes that are frustrated with their current workout and not getting the results they are seeking.

Identifying your ideal customer is thinking of the conversations that problem would present. Aim to put yourself in a prospective customers shoes and really analyze what the desired solution or result would be. How might that customer need to have that solution or result marketed to them? Knowing as much as possible about those problems will help you better communicate the conversations related to those problems. Your products and services are only as good as what you know about the people you are helping. The better you can relate with these conversations through your marketing the easier it will be to convince customers to buy your solution.

How Do You Do What You Do?

The understanding is in the details, once you settle on what it is that you do, the next thing people will want to know is how. This is where your product and services should come in to shine. You want your products and services to give a result, benefit or provide a solution through whatever it is that you do. What are some ways you can create a product or service that delivers these desired outcomes?

Here is an example:

A personal trainer that helps people gain muscle mass would promote a workout they have specifically formulated for that purpose. The formatted workout is the solution and also delivers a certain result which is the gaining of muscle mass. The personal trainer helps people gain muscle mass, how they do it is by instructing the client through a specially formatted workout created for that result.

Here is another example:

A fashion designer that specializes in creating custom fit dresses. The designer might promote her free consultation service where she is to gather the details needed to create the custom dress giving a tailored experience for the client. The solution the designer provides is custom tailoring the end result is a dress that the client knows they will be able to fit. The designer specializes in creating custom fit dresses, how the designer does this is by engaging in a free consultation with the client to gather the details needed to create the dress.

The way you explain the how behind what you do can result in gaining a new customer or create confusion and having missed the opportunity to gain a new customer. Become confident on the best way to concisely and clearly say how you do what you do. It will offer additional details beyond the What Do You Do? It will engage those who are interested into further conversation and can even result in a sale. Direct questions about your brand are an opportunity to create conversations about how you do what you do. These are the conversations that put you in a position to convert an inquirer to a customer.

How to Discover Your Target Audience

A **target audience** is a particular segment of consumers within a predetermined target market, identified as targets for a particular advertisement or message. After completing the process of deciphering a Brand Personality Code you will have clarity on exactly who your target audience is. Each step helps to cultivate your brand's identity and image so that you can correctly identify the solution or result you provide. Once you understand what result or solution you provide you can then address the conversations surrounding the problems that customers would desire solutions or results for. Then the following step would be to confirm your products or services align with the desired solution or result. Brand marketing is the bait to out people who are best suited for your product or service. Use the feedback from marketing to identify and document the similarities, demographics, age, location, education, and socioeconomic status associated with the conversations and problems you have discussed.

Marketing is ongoing so it will require periodically fine tuning your approach based on customer feedback, sales data, and marketing data. The benefit of marketing to your target audience is that you will be able to market more efficiently and effectively. Instead of just spending money to try and accommodate a wide range of consumers you can start with focusing on a particular group. Starting out it can be tempting to want to serve everyone, but have you ever heard of the phrase "Jack of all trades, master of none?. Well, there is an advantage to being the expert when it comes to serving a particular demographic of people. Directing focus on a small or special segment of an audience can also position you to market a high performing **Unique Selling Position** or USP. This approach may seem rather limiting however do not write it off just yet. A brand can have a target audience and also serve other groups of people. Targeted marketing is a strategic move to market to and focus directly on those people who have a higher potential to be converted to customers, rather than to expend efforts over a vast group. As your brand gains credibility in serving a target audience you can and should look for other aligning and relevant audiences to begin to target and serve.

In conclusion, your marketing strategy should be strategic and progressive.

If your goals are ambitious, then look to gradually scale over time. Identifying multiple target audiences will create more revenue for your brand and allow for innovative and forward moving ideas to develop. As a precaution consider take caution in being overzealous and focusing on one target audience or two extremely different audiences. Doing so can possibly cause you to handicap the evolution of your brand. It is not uncommon to feel as though you have hit the "sweet spot" or feeling like your product/service is for everyone. Remember your Brand Personality Code and revisit it at least once a year to remain focused on your identity, image,marketing, inspirations, goals, and objectives that illustrate the vision of your brand.

The Marketing Cycle

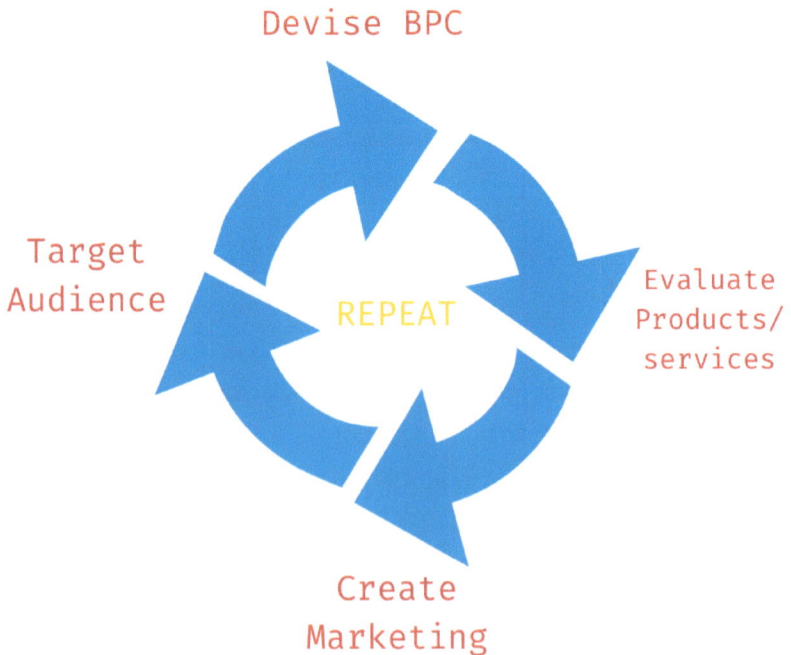

Devise BPC

Target Audience

REPEAT

Evaluate Products/ services

Create Marketing

How to Craft Your Elevator Pitch

Now that we have discussed the Brand Personality Code, I want to explain to how to write a simple elevator pitch. An **elevator pitch** is a short 10, 30, or 60 second message that conveys your Brand Personality Code. It says who you are, what you do, who you help, and how you do it. A version including all or a few of these steps can be used to create your brand's elevator pitch. Depending on the nature of your business it may vary as to what you might include in your pitch. Go with what is most effective and what works best to express your brand. If you really want to knock it out of the park, your brand's pitch can include components such as mentioning negative emotions experienced, ideal client description, results they want, your solution and the benefits.

Ideally the reason you might want to have an elevator pitch to recite is so that when you speak with prospective customers or perhaps an investor, you can quickly and concisely tell them what they need to know about your brand without dumping too much information on them. The goal is to convey what they need to know and garner interest that leads to a conversation that leads to a sale or a new client. A pitch can be used when networking online, at networking events, job interviews, prospective client meetings, regular client meetings and other spaces where potential customers may be present.

Here are the steps to creating a pitch:

Step 1 Gather the answers from your Brand Personality Code (to create pitch)

Who are you?

What do you do?

Who do you help?

How do you do it?

Step 2 Construct the pitch like this:

1. **I/We-** Use these pronouns or your brand name, occupation, industry etc. if applicable. **(use the Who are You?)**
2. **Help/teach/support/assist-** use the applicable verb for what you do. **(use the What do you do?)**

3. **Ideal client description**- say who it is you help. For ex. Stressed moms, frustrated athletes, overwhelmed shoppers. It is best to be as specific as possible with your description. **(use the Who do you help?)**

4. **Solution**- what is the solution or result that is provided or achieved? For example: creating a solution, discover a problem, put their needs first, realize the best solution **(use the How do you do it?)**

How to Craft a Pitch	
I/We (Who are You)	Use these pronouns or use your name or company name and occupation, industry etc. if applicable.
Help/teach (What do you do?)	use the applicable verb for what you do.
Ideal Client (Who do you help?)	say who it is you help. For ex. Stressed moms, frustrated athletes. It is best to be as specific as possible with your description.
Solution (How do you do it?)	solution or result that is provided achieved. For example, creating a solution, discover a problem, put their needs first,

Recalling the examples I used earlier in this chapter here are two hypothetical pitches that I constructed to demonstrate how this looks.

Example #1 Personal Trainer

I am Tania, a personal trainer that assists frustrated athletes by creating personalized objective workout plans.

Example#2 Esthetician

I am James an esthetician who helps stressed mothers rediscover their beauty.

To write an even better elevator pitch add more detail to the solution that describes a benefit. This will give your prospective customers further information about your brand and pique interest.

Example #1 Personal Trainer -Pitch 2

I am Tania a personal trainer that assists frustrated athletes by creating personalized objective workout plans that help them achieve the specific results they want.

Example#2 Esthetician- Pitch 2

I am James an esthetician who helps stressed mothers rediscover their beauty by offering skin care treatments to remove stress lines making them look and feel younger.

You do not have to follow the exact format as outlined when crafting your brand's elevator pitch. Use words and phrases that do the best job of getting your message across. The BPC (Brand Personality Code) and pitch template serve as a guide to help you effectively communicate your brands purpose to your audience. To deliver a successful pitch, speak with enthusiasm, make eye contact, and be aware of body language cues that you are sending and receiving. Most importantly recall and connect with the excitement and passion you have for your brand and always remember your why!

Chapter 4: 3 Brand Success Fundamentals

Thus far we have discussed the specifics of marketing and branding. Together these components exude a set of expectations, feelings, thoughts, experiences, emotions and ideas associated with a brand. These concepts are what contribute to the complexities of marketing and branding. However, with strategic planning, testing, and optimization a highly successful brand can be produced.

Today one can easily observe the footprints of success left behind by other top performing brands. It would be wise to note the methods and techniques that are commonly demonstrated and apply them uniquely to your own brand. Some key characteristics involved in brand success are consistency, authenticity, and trustworthiness. After looking further into researching myself, I found that there are three key fundamentals that exist in top perfoming brands today.

These three things are:

1. **A unique selling position.**
2. **A transfer of value.**
3. **A compelling story/message.**

Unique Selling Position (USP)

The characteristics of a strong unique selling position involve the ability to tactfully convey a benefit and solve a problem. Establishing a unique selling position is a reflection of the focus and direction of a brand's marketing. The Brand Personality code mentioned before in the previous chapter, uncovers the unique selling position when the questions "what do you do?" and "how do you do it?" are answered. Combine these answers along with the answers for "who do you help?" and "who are you?" to construct a strong unique selling position. A USP is your brands promise to deliver a specific result, experience, solution, or benefit. It should effectively embody the value that your brand is committed to offering.

Transfer of Value

Customers are always looking for the value in everything they give their time, attentioin and money to. As a brand providing that value is going to get you a customer for life, not just for the short-term. Understanding what the customer values will help you to connect with them and fulfill their needs accordingly. Listen to feedback enables your brand to create the greatest sense of value for your audience. Find small ways to go above and beyond for your customers to compel loyalty. Additionally, providing helpful information to your customers can position your brand as an authority in your industry. Through the customers eyes, you are then viewed as a credible and trustworthy source. It creates a gateway for them to continue participating, interacting, and making purchases with your brand for many years to come.

A compelling story/message

A brand's story or message is most commonly tied to how the company was founded or created. Usually the story or message revolves around overcoming a conflict. Then finally having created or come across a resolution to that conflict. The story or message is used to effectively communicate the vision and mission of your brand. It relays the general facts about the brand, its values, its philosophy, emotional connection, and its passions. It tells people why they should pay attention or even care about the brand's presence in the first place. Compelling stories and messages allow current and future customers to share in the experience, relate with a story of their own, and create fulfilling conversations that lead to a sense of community, trust and loyalty within your brand. Make use of the Brand Personality Code to construct your brand's compelling story or message.

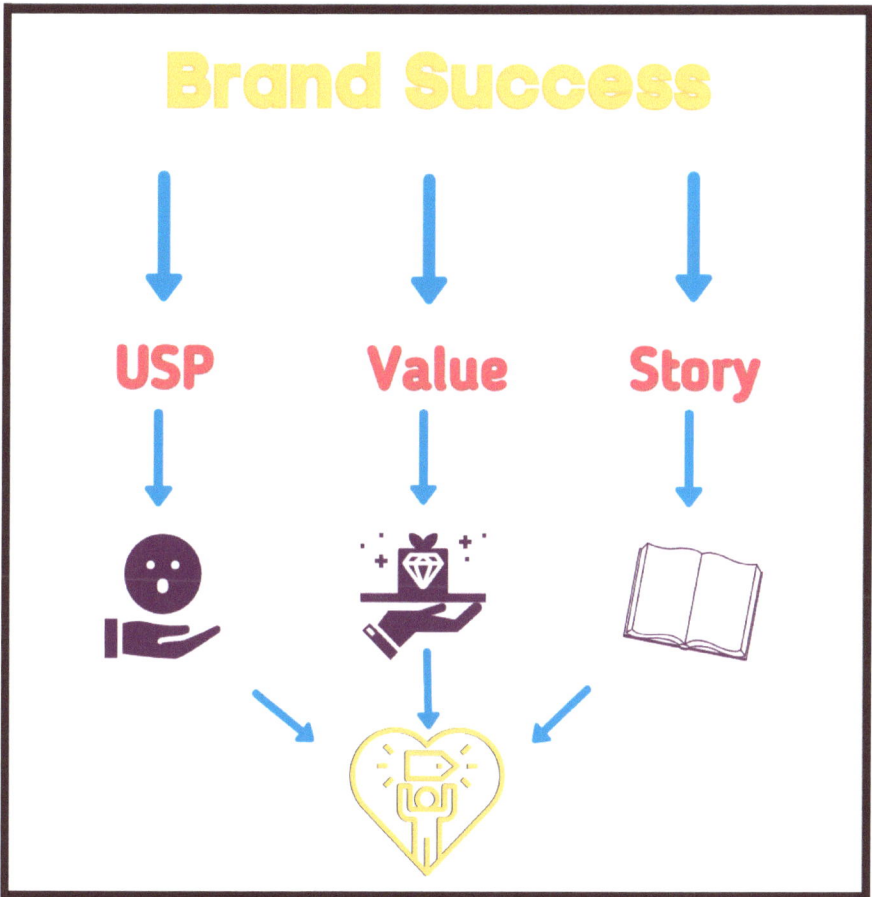

By combining and building on these three fundamentals you will solidify a strong brand presence. Be consistent with aligning and incorporating these fundamentals within your overall branding and marketing strategies. Always uphold your brand's vision, voice, and mission. Make it a priority to express it in every kind of communication utilized. Use your brand story, message, value, and USP as a starting point to generate and cultivate ideas. These ideas can serve as the blueprint for devising strategic and compelling marketing campaigns. Opening the door for higher brand awareness, attracting new customers, introducing new products, and strengthening current customer relationships.

6

Chapter 5: Providing Value Through Marketing

D elivering value through marketing is an essential criterion to truly connect with your audience. Value is intangible and can be perceived in a number of ways. In reference to brand consumption, it can be explained as the customer's perception relating to the price or benefits of a product or service. In another way, it can also be the specific way information is presented that empowers the consumer to make informed decisions.

To create value, it is important to understand what is actually valuable to your audience. How they want to feel, who they want to be, and what they want most are all tied to their desires and motivations. People will often support brands whose values are intricately connected to their own. Take note of what values your target audience holds and find a way to connect it to your brand's values. A brand that is conscientious to its marketing will know if it is the product received or the experience had that shapes the value for their customers. Other factors to consider is how your products or services are viewed when it comes to competitors in the market. How does your offer compare to what is already available and are you sub par, on par, or above average? Evaluate your competitors to see where you can improve and continue to prioritize creating exceptional value for your customers. Aim to provide the most value for what they pay, not necessarily how much they pay. To achieve a solution or result that delivers a feeling they want, helps them be who they want, or gives them what they want, the cost can be higher as long as the value is sufficient.

Value is synonymous with worth, so decide on how you will demonstrate your brand's worth through the value you provide and do it in an exceptional way. Understand what your customers find valuable and position your brand to produce products and services that meet their needs. Give your business a competitive and innovative edge by presenting customers with products and services that meet their demands.

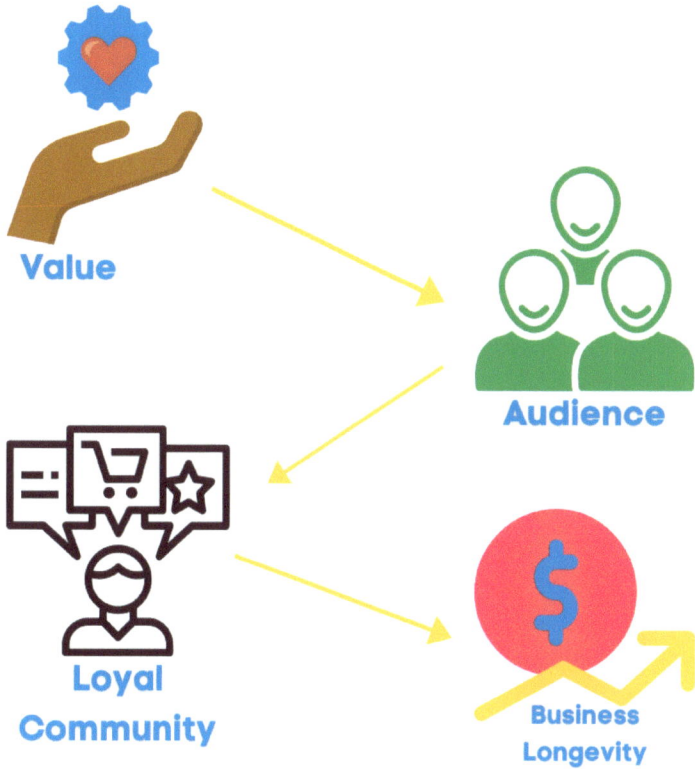

To garner interest and consistent attention to your brand deliver valuable content within your marketing. People are more likely to make confident buying decisions when they are better informed. Buyers are always looking for information on the best products, services, and brands for their problems. They research constantly on the pros and cons of many services and products often having "**analysis paralysis**" which slows down the buying process. Taking this into consideration, it makes a lot of sense as to why so many brands are creating content as a strategy to market and expedite the buying process of their products or services. The key is to create quality content that discusses the problems and concerns associated with your products, services, brand, or industry. Some of the most popular forms of quality content are informative blog posts, informative or entertaining videos, do's and don'ts checklists and more. It creates an opportunity to be a prominent voice or authority within your industry. A derivative to the benefits of establishing authority is loyalty to your brand. Make a conscious and genuine effort to distribute quality content consistently in order to establish a strong relationship with your audience and build trust. Once that trust is obtained the audience sees your brand as an authority, and you will be able to sell your products and services to them more successfully.

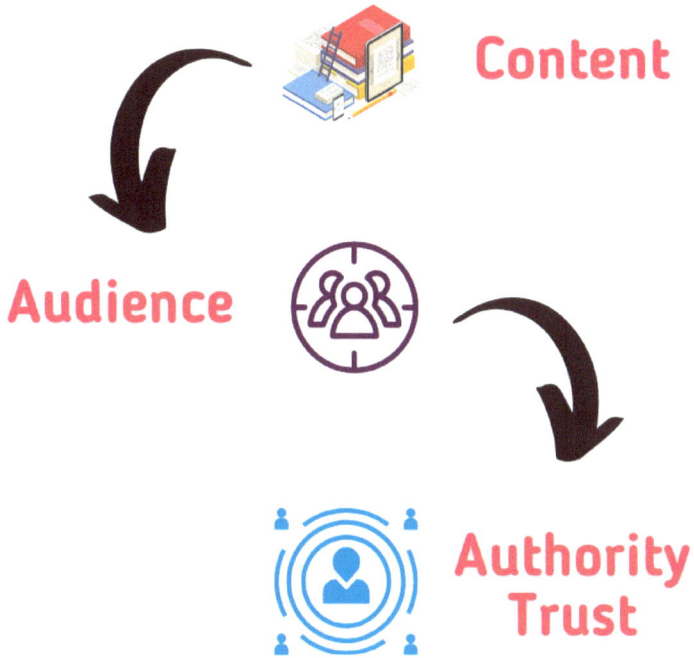

7

Chapter 6: How to Implement Marketing

S o far we have discussed marketing, branding, the Brand Personality Code, brand success fundamentals and value. Now it is time to discuss how it all comes together implement it into a sound plan for marketing. Let's discuss planning out a marketing strategy which means defining clear goals and desired outcomes. Your strategy will include a plan to attract and retain customers and exactly what you will do to market your products and services. If possible, include research, prior performance data and possible ideas for strategies in the future. A marketing strategy is a necessity that will assist you in putting all ideas and research in one place.

While completing this process you will :

- Define a core message that shapes your brand's overall style, vision, and voice.
- Set a budget that aligns with your goals.
- Achieve a higher return on investment by tracking processes and collecting data to optimize campaigns.
- Gain clarity on what is and is not working, plan better strategies, and generate better ideas.
- Remain organized and focused throughout your marketing process.

Some opportunistic times to consider crafting a marketing strategy are:

- At the end of the year.
- When launching new products or services.
- When starting a new business.
- When you have no strategy.

Being proactive about constructing a marketing strategy ensures you are ready for the new year, understand how to capture your markets, and have clear direction on how you plan to grow and scale your brand. There is no definitive time to use a marketing strategy. If there is an absence of a strategy, then it is time to make one.

Where to Start

If you have an established brand, then simply start by making a record of what you have already tried. Review your history and recall any marketing strategies you may have implemented and use them as a reference to build your new strategy. Document this information in a more organized way like using a word document or spreadsheet document. Try to include as many details as possible such as investments made, time allocated, dates, and duration of campaigns. If you are completely new or have not done any type of marketing these ten steps are the best place to start for you as well.

10 Steps to Build Your Marketing Strategy

Building your marketing strategy can be an intimidating task. No need to sweat it, you are not the first nor will you be the last person to complete such a task. Here is an outline to follow and establish a marketing strategy for your brand.

1. Define your offers.
2. Define your brand message.

3. Define your target audience.
4. Research Market and Competitors.
5. Define your brand USP.
6. Outline your goals.
7. Outline your marketing strategy.
8. Decide on a budget.
9. Decide on marketing tactics.
10. Define metrics and KPIs.

Now let'sgo through the steps and discuss the context of what each one entails.

- **Define your offer.**

Before moving forward to map out your strategy it is imperative to define your products and services. Create an outline and provide the features, how the features benefit customers, what makes your offers different, and the price.

- **Define your brand message.**

Once you establish what you are selling, you will want to explain why you are selling it. Establish what you want to accomplish with your brand. Think about how why you want to help your customers. What are the things that make your products or services important and why should people buy from you instead of competing companies?

- **Define your target audience.**

After establishing what you sell and why you are selling it, you now need to confirm who you sell to. A way to simplify this process and make it less cumbersome is to create an ideal customer. Creating an ideal customer describes your target audience by outlining things such as demographics, professional details, psychology, goals, problems, and influences.

Defining Your Target Audience	
Demographics	age, gender, income, education, location,
Professional Details	industry, job title, company
Psychographics	personality traits, beliefs, attitudes,
Goals, Challenges, Influences	what they what to achieve,pain points, what they are afraid of or in need of,favorite media outlets, thought leaders,

- **Research Market and Competitors.**

It is important to be aware of what is going on in the market. You do not want to be behind or subpar when it comes to what you are offering. Research your market and competitors so you are not blindly entering the market. Research on your market will answer questions such as how big the market is, how many brands you will be competing with, what the trends are, how much customers are willing to pay, what businesses have similar offerings, and what the sales cycle looks like. The answers to these will be the key to understanding the environment in which your brand will compete.

Your research will answer questions like who your competitors are, how big they are, their strengths, weaknesses, unique selling position, so that you can you differentiate your brand.

- **Define your brand USP.**

Once you reach this step you will have enough information about your brand, market and competitors. Use this information to decide how you will position your brand in the market. Declare your unique selling position, highlight outstanding features, specify your target market, and Brand Personality Code.

- **Outline your goals.**

Define your long and short-term goals. Give thought to where you are starting at and where you want to be in 3, 5, or 10 years. Some examples of marketing goals are to attract customers, increase website traffic, increase sales, increase following on social media, generate more leads and improve online presence.

- **Outline your marketing strategy.**

Your marketing strategy will be the roadmap to reaching your goals. From here you can determine what marketing tactics are best suited that align with the goals you want to reach. Some examples include online advertising, email marketing, print advertising, social media networking, and blogging.

- **Decide on a budget.**

Depending on where you are in your business journey there will be some factors that dictate the size of your marketing budget. Once you have made it this far in the process you will have the information you need to decide on a budget. A few things that will need to be considered are your current revenue, if you will dedicate a percentage of profits to marketing, the amount you will need to invest in marketing, and what type of marketing budget competitors might have.

- **Decide on marketing tactics.**

The next step is to create some ideas as to what you may be able to offer to appeal to potential customers. Offers such as special deals, rewards or samples can be a great starting point. Examples of ways to initiate marketing campaigns are business cards, online marketing with use of web ads, and email marketing.

- **Define metrics and KPIs**

One last step in your marketing strategy is deciding what metrics you will use to evaluate the success of your campaigns. There are varying options available and it depends on what information is most valuable and beneficial to helping your brand grow. Types of information that is valuable are how much you spend to get a new customer, what percentage of customers you have compared to the whole market of customers and whether or not that number is growing. Having the correct metrics will ensure that you can make informed decisions when determining how you will spend your marketing budget.

Overview

This concludes the ten step outline for creating your brand's marketing strategy. Go through each step and make your own list of notes. Use this outline to devise your best strategy, revisit it a few days later and continue to make necessary revisions and improvements. Be sure to ask questions to an honest family member or friend for input and to check your thinking. Sometimes you can get very self-absorbed in your brand and dismiss opporunities to identify a target audience, a need or recognize helpful constrasting perspectives.

As a reminder, remember that you do not have to do all the thinking yourself! Learn from competitors and other industries. Study trends and use the information you find to produce or add flair to your own ideas. In most cases there will exist many tried and true methods that you can also adopt in your strategy. Stay focused but also remain open to any changes that may require you to update and adjust your strategy. Changes that can impact your marketing can be things such as unexpected rapid growth or changes in competition and overall market. In these cases, some revision may be needed but remain true to your overall goals that you outline in your marketing strategy.

8

Outcome

Congratulations! You made it to the end of the handbook. If any confusion existed on where to begin with your marketing, I sincerely hope that at this point you have gained the clarity and confidence needed to plan your strategy moving forward. Creating great brand marketing is an immensely essential component of brand success. It helps to relay your Brand Personality Code, vision, and voice of your brand to the world. We all start our brands for many different reasons and have our own personal "whys" behind what we choose to pursue and create. That is what makes creating a brand so exciting and fulfilling. It is an opportunity to bring the dream or the "why" to life and see other people connect with your brand in their own unique way coming together for support, cause, or community.

For most freelancers, entreprenuers and startups, marketing is the last component considered when constructing a brand. Marketing is one of the aspects of a brand that can be just as fun and enjoyable as the creation. Marketing does not have to follow traditional or conventional methods by any means. So many brands are breaking the mold by showing their true colors and authentic flairs. Think about how you want to leave your footprint on the world and allow yourself to creatively craft marketing that will reflect your vision in its full capacity.

Take your time to fully receive the information contained within this book. It is a lot of information and it takes some time to absorb. This is why I did not go extremely in depth with this book. There is so much more information I wanted to share pertaining to solidifying brand success. However, for this particular book, my goal was to cover the basic information that can be followed easily and help my fellow Tycoons confidently go out and market their brands.

Once you have taken the time to fully receive the information please use it! Get yourself a pen, notebook, and carefully go through each chapter, take detailed notes, do the worksheets and create your amazing marketing strategy for your brand. You have everything you need contained in this book and I am excited to see what you will do with it. I as well as the world (they just don't know it yet!) are waiting on the next brand that will impact us in the most incredible way. I have a feeling it might be yours, so prove me right!

To your success,
 Marquetta Hewitt
 Creative Entrepreneur

9

Glossary

Advertising- the business of preparing advertisements for publication or broadcast.

Analysis Paralysis- a process when overanalyzing or overthinking a situation can cause forward motion or decision-making to become "paralyzed", meaning that no solution or course of action is decided upon.

Brand- the symbol, name, term, design, or any other features that uniquely identifies and distinguishes a company.

Brand Culture- the sense of lifestyle, habits, and etiquette associated with your brand and the people who are a part of it.

Brand Identity- the visible aspects of your brand such as the logo, color scheme, and design.

Brand Image- the impression of your product and brand that current or future customers have.

Brand Marketing- the theory and tactics used to promote your brand overall by giving value to the customer.

Brand Personality Code- The equation that entails what a brand does, who they are, who they serve, how they serve.

Brand Story- commonly tied to how a company was founded or created. Usually revolving around a conflict and resolution or solution being uncovered. It may also express the company's vision and mission.

Business Coach- an individual of experience and knowledge that helps facilitate the learning and implementation of various business solutions and concepts.

Customer Acquisition- the process of finding and persuading prospective customers to buy from your business in a way that is both measurable and repeatable.

Customer Retention- the ability of a company or product to retain its customers over some specified period.

Content Marketing- creating, publishing, and distributing content in the form of videos, written format, and audio format to promote and sell a product or service.

Digital Marketing- using online based technology such as computers and phones to promote and sell a product or service.

Direct Response Marketing- a method of marketing relies on an immediate response to an offer presented through advertising.

Elevator Pitch- a short 10, 30, or 60 second message that conveys your Brand Personality Code.

Entrepreneur- one who organizes, manages, and assumes the risks of a business or enterprise.

Equity- is ownership of assets that may have debts or other liabilities attached to them.

Freelancer- a person who pursues a profession without a long-term commitment to any one employer.

Ideal Client- See Target Audience

Influencer Marketing- collaborating with a well-known authoritative individual or brand to promote your product or service.

Key Performance Indicator (KPI)- Key performance indicators (KPIs) are a set of performance measurements that demonstrate how effectively an organization is achieving key objectives.

Marketing- actions a company takes to promote the buying and or selling of a product or service.

Marketing Strategy- a plan of action to promote or sell a product or service.

Offer- a presentation of a product or service with a proposed benefit in order to obtain a sale or valuable information.

Revenue- the total income produced by a given source.

Startup- a company that is in the initial stages of business. Until the business gets off the ground, a startup is often financed by its founders and may attempt to attract outside investment

Target Audience- is a particular segment of consumers within a predetermined target market, identified as targets for a particular advertisement or message.

Targeted Marketing- the process of identifying customers and promoting products and services via mediums that are likely to reach those potential customers.

Tycoon- a businessperson of exceptional wealth, power, and influence.

Unique Selling Position- a promise to deliver a specific result, experience, solution, or benefit. It should effectively embody the value that your brand is committed to offering.

Value- the customer's perception relating to the price or benefits of a product or service.

About the Author

Marquetta is a Florida native from Panama City, Florida. She grew up an army brat and attended Southern University A&M College majoring in Biology. She later went on to spend a few years in Alaska where she created the blog "The Magnificent Tycoon" and also established her record label The Matriarchal Collective. She enjoys writing, producing and recording music, traveling, hiking, and spending time with close family and friends. She creates content to help entreprenuer-minded individuals excel in building superior brands. In addition to her book she offers online courses, webinars, and video content. She is also a vegetarian and an advocate for spirituality and self-awareness.

You can connect with me on:

🌐 https://sauceytycoon.com
f https://facebook.com/mhewittcoach

www.ingramcontent.com/pod-product-compliance
Lightning Source LLC
Chambersburg PA
CBHW041716200326
41519CB00005B/276